LOOK AND FIND®

Disney's little einsteins™

Illustrated by Dean Kleven
Photos by Getty Images, Corbis, iStock Photos, and Photos.com
Tabla Drum © Anthony Hall, Harmonium © Umbar Shakir, Mongoose © Nico Smit
Written by Caleb Burroughs

Published by Louis Weber, C.E.O., Publications International, Ltd.
7373 North Cicero Avenue, Lincolnwood, Illinois 60712
Ground Floor, 59 Gloucester Place, London W1U 8JJ

Customer Service: 1-800-595-8484 or customer_service@pilbooks.com

www.pilbooks.com

Manufactured in China.

8 7 6 5 4 3 2 1

ISBN-13: 978-1-4127-6795-8
ISBN-10: 1-4127-6795-4

publications international, ltd.

Hello! I'm Leo and this is June, Annie, Quincy, and our friend Rocket. We're the Little Einsteins. We are going to New York to put on a big musical show. But first we have to travel the world in Rocket to find the instruments and props that we'll need. Will you help us find these things to help us on our big trip?

This suitcase

Globe

Canteen

Map

Compass

Camera

Aloha from Hawaii! On these islands of sand and sun, there are many musical things. Will you look for these Hawaiian musical instruments?

Ipu Heke

Pahu

Steel guitar

Kâ `eke `eke

Ukulele

Pû

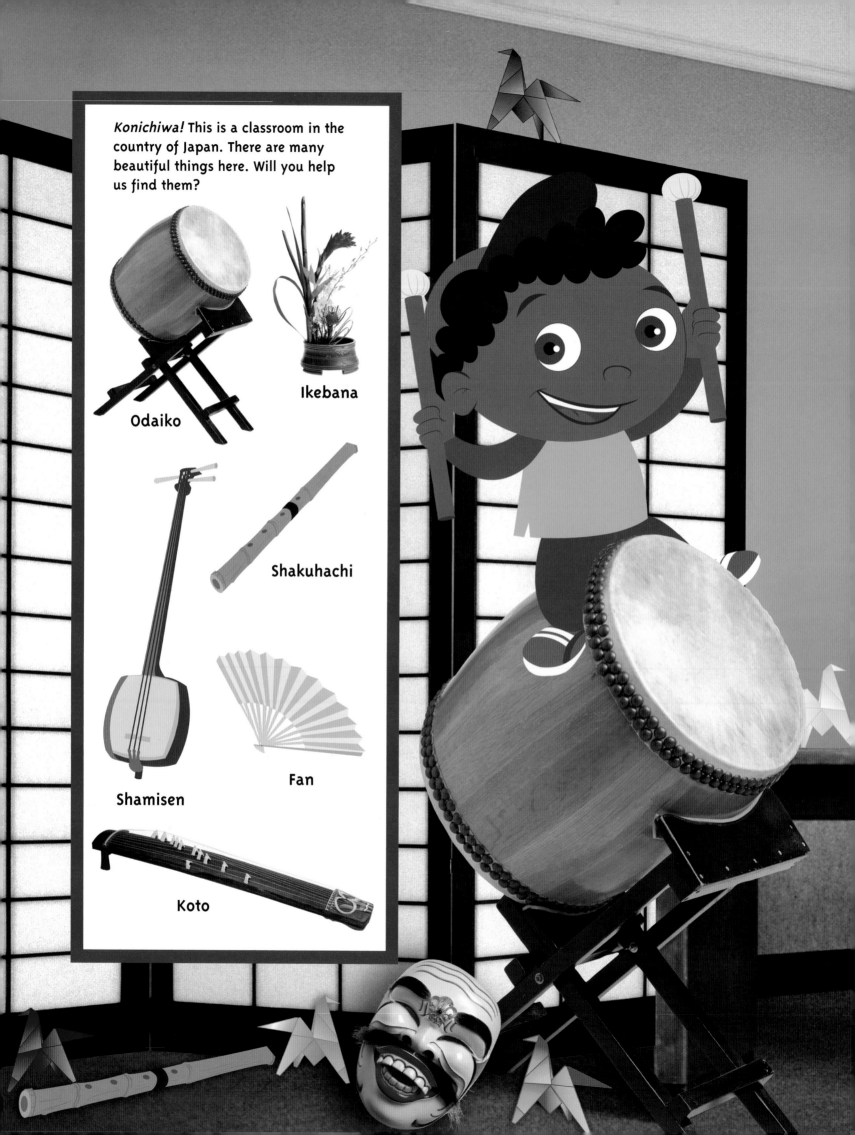

Konichiwa! This is a classroom in the country of Japan. There are many beautiful things here. Will you help us find them?

Odaiko

Ikebana

Shakuhachi

Shamisen

Fan

Koto

Namaste! Welcome to India. The big, beautiful building you see is the Taj Mahal. Look around for these Indian instruments that are outside.

Mridanga

Harmonium

Sitar

Tanpura

Tabla

Shehnai

Ciao! We are rehearsing for a big performance in a fancy Italian opera house. Will you look for these instruments and musical objects that will make our show even better?

Sheet music

Conductor's baton

Oboe

Violin

Harp

Trumpet

Guten Tag! Welcome to Germany. We're here in this mountain meadow for a polka party. Will you help us find these musical instruments so we can polka?

Accordion

Fiddle

Hammered dulcimer

Tuba

Upright bass

Bass drum

We are on safari in Africa. Not only are there many animals here, but many musical instruments and art objects, too. Look and find these African things around the hot and grassy plains.

Whistle

Kalimba

Mask

Rain stick

Drum

Marimba

We have finally completed our mission! Rocket is flying to New York City. We can use all of the things we found to put on a musical show! Look for these instruments we found on our adventures.

Shehnai

Bass drum

Bassoon

Ukulele

African drum

Koto

Return to the Little Einsteins' clubhouse to find these things in the backyard:

- ◯ Butterfly
- ◯ Squirrel
- ◯ Grasshopper
- ◯ Bird
- ◯ Rabbit
- ◯ Purple flower

Surf back to Hawaii and find these Hawaiian objects:

- ◯ Lei
- ◯ Grass hula skirt
- ◯ Surfboard
- ◯ Traditional boat
- ◯ Pineapple
- ◯ Coconut

Jet back to Japan and look for origami birds of these different colors:

- ◯ Red
- ◯ Pink
- ◯ Orange
- ◯ Purple
- ◯ White
- ◯ Yellow

Return to India and look for these animals that live there:

- ◯ Elephant
- ◯ Tiger
- ◯ Brahma bull
- ◯ Cobra
- ◯ Mongoose
- ◯ Monkey

Drum your way back to Italy and find these percussion instruments:

- ⃝ **Bass drum**
- ⃝ **Gong**
- ⃝ **Bells**
- ⃝ **Timpani drum**
- ⃝ **Triangle**
- ⃝ **Xylophone**

Polka back to the mountains and help the Little Einsteins look for these popular German things:

- ⃝ **German Shepherd dogs**
- ⃝ **Three loaves of bread**
- ⃝ **Zeppelin**
- ⃝ **Alpine walking stick**
- ⃝ **Cuckoo clock**
- ⃝ **Sausage**

Trek to Africa to find these different animals:

- ⃝ **Cape buffalo**
- ⃝ **Lion**
- ⃝ **Zebra**
- ⃝ **Giraffe**
- ⃝ **Vulture**
- ⃝ **Elephant**

Look inside Rocket's cockpit for things we found on our mission:

- ⃝ **Cuckoo clock**
- ⃝ **African mask**
- ⃝ **Japanese fan**
- ⃝ **Steel guitar**
- ⃝ **Sheet music**
- ⃝ **Sitar**

Can you go back and find Rocket in every scene?